TEDDY

by Tristan Bernays

Music by Dougal Irvine

samuelfrench.co.uk

Copyright © 2018 by Tristan Bernays (book and lyrics)
and Dougal Irvine (music)
All Rights Reserved

TEDDY is fully protected under the copyright laws of the British Commonwealth, including Canada, the United States of America, and all other countries of the Copyright Union. All rights, including professional and amateur stage productions, recitation, lecturing, public reading, motion picture, radio broadcasting, television and the rights of translation into foreign languages are strictly reserved.

ISBN 978-0-573-11551-6

www.samuelfrench.co.uk
www.samuelfrench.com

For Amateur Production Enquiries

United Kingdom and World
excluding north america
plays@samuelfrench.co.uk
020 7255 4302/01

Each title is subject to availability from Samuel French,
depending upon country of performance.

CAUTION: Professional and amateur producers are hereby warned that *TEDDY* is subject to a licensing fee. Publication of this play does not imply availability for performance. Both amateurs and professionals considering a production are strongly advised to apply to the appropriate agent before starting rehearsals, advertising, or booking a theatre. A licensing fee must be paid whether the title is presented for charity or gain and whether or not admission is charged.

The Professional Rights in this play are controlled by Knight Hall Agency Ltd, 7 Mallow St, London EC1Y 8RQ.

The Professional Rights in the music are controlled by Berlin Associates, 7 Tyers Gate, London SE1 3HX and

No one shall make any changes in this title for the purpose of production. No part of this book may be reproduced, stored in a retrieval system, or transmitted in any form, by any means, now known or yet to be invented, including mechanical, electronic, photocopying, recording, videotaping, or otherwise, without the prior written permission of the publisher. No one shall upload this title, or part of this title, to any social media websites.

The right of Tristan Bernays to be identified as author and Dougal Irvine to be identified as composer of this work has been asserted in accordance with Section 77 of the Copyright, Designs and Patents Act 1988.

THINKING ABOUT PERFORMING A SHOW?

There are thousands of plays and musicals available to perform from Samuel French right now, and applying for a licence is easier and more affordable than you might think

From classic plays to brand new musicals, from monologues to epic dramas, there are shows for everyone.

Plays and musicals are protected by copyright law so if you want to perform them, the first thing you'll need is a licence. This simple process helps support the playwright by ensuring they get paid for their work, and means that you'll have the documents you need to stage the show in public.

Not all our shows are available to perform all the time, so it's important to check and apply for a licence before you start rehearsals or commit to doing the show.

LEARN MORE & FIND THOUSANDS OF SHOWS

Browse our full range of plays and musicals and find out more about how to license a show

www.samuelfrench.co.uk/perform

Talk to the friendly experts in our Licensing team for advice on choosing a show, and help with licensing

plays@samuelfrench.co.uk   020 7387 9373

Acting Editions
BORN TO PERFORM

Playscripts designed from the ground up to work the way you do in rehearsal, performance and study

---

Larger, clearer text for easier reading

Wider margins for notes

Performance features such as character and props lists, sound and lighting cues, and more

---

+ CHOOSE A SIZE AND STYLE TO SUIT YOU

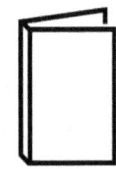 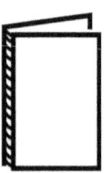 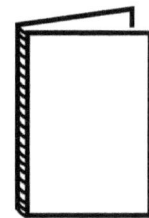

STANDARD EDITION

Our regular paperback book at our regular size

SPIRAL-BOUND EDITION

The same size as the Standard Edition, but with a sturdy, easy-to-fold, easy-to-hold spiral-bound spine

LARGE EDITION

A4 size and spiral bound, with larger text and a blank page for notes opposite every page of text. Perfect for technical and directing use

---

| LEARN MORE | samuelfrench.co.uk/actingeditions

MUSIC USE NOTE

The music parts for this title are available on hire to licensed productions from Samuel French. Fees and conditions of this hire are quoted on application.

Sample materials are available on request for perusal prior to application.

USE OF COPYRIGHT MUSIC

A licence issued by Samuel French Ltd to perform this play does not include permission to use the incidental music specified in this copy.

Where the place of performance is already licensed by the PERFORMING RIGHT SOCIETY (PRS) a return of the music used must be made to them. If the place of performance is not so licensed then application should be made to the PRS, 2 Pancras Square, London, N1C 4AG.

A separate and additional licence from
PHONOGRAPHIC PERFORMANCE LTD,
1 Upper James Street, London W1F 9DE (www.ppluk.com) is needed whenever commercial recordings are used.

IMPORTANT BILLING AND CREDIT REQUIREMENTS

If you have obtained performance rights to this title, please refer to your licensing agreement for important billing and credit requirements.

ABOUT THE AUTHOR

Tristan is an award-winning writer and performer from London. His work has been performed at The Globe, Soho Theatre, Bush Theatre, National Theatre Studio and Southwark Playhouse.

His work includes: *Old Fools* (Southwark Playhouse, 2018, Dir: Sharon Burrell); *Teddy* (The Vaults + UK Tour, 2018, Dir: Eleanor Rhode); *Boudica* (Shakespeare's Globe, 2017, Dir: Eleanor Rhode); *Frankenstein* (Wiltons Music Hall, 2017, Dir: Eleanor Rhode); *Testament* (VAULT Festival, 2017, Dir: Lucy Jane Atkinson); *Teddy* (Southwark Playhouse, 2015, Dir: Eleanor Rhode) and *The Bread & the Beer* (Soho Theatre + UK Tour, 2014, Dir: Sophie Larsmon).

Reviews for previous work:

"Tristan Bernays has created a dementia parable that somehow moves and finds light in the deterioration of the mind – through love" ★★★★ *Independent* on *Old Fools*
   (Nominated for Best New Play from the Off West End Theatre Awards 2018)

"Gina McKee reigns supreme" ★★★★ *Guardian* on *Boudica*

"Energy and invention abound. Remarkable" ★★★★ *Evening Standard* on *Teddy*
   (Winner of Best New Musical at the Off West End Theatre Awards 2016)

"WOW ...one of the most action-packed dynamic shows of the Fringe" ★★★★ *The Scotsman* on *The Bread & the Beer*

Tristan is Writer In Residence at Dancing Ledge Productions and was also a member of the Bush Theatre's Emerging Writers Group 2016/17.

www.tristanbernays.com / @tristanbernays

ABOUT THE COMPOSER

Dougal is an award winning writer, lyricist and composer.

Credits as Playwright: *Memoirs of an Asian Football Casual* (Curve).

As Writer/Lyricist/Composer: *Eric Idle's Adventures of The Owl and the Pussycat* (Belgrade Theatre/Selladoor), *The Buskers Opera* (Park Theatre – The Stage top ten new musicals 2016), *Angry Birds* (The Space, Havering), *The Other School* (St James Theatre/NYMT), *In Touch* (Bridewell Theatre) and *Departure Lounge* (LONDON Waterloo East, Public Theatre – WhatsonStage Award Nominee, Best New Musical. MTN Award Winner, Best Music. OFF BROADWAY, NY Summer Play Festival).

As Lyricist: *Laila* (Rifco Arts/Watford Palace) and *Britain's Got Bhangra* (Rifco Arts/Stratford East/Watford Palace. Two national tours – UK Theatre Award nominee, Best Musical. Off West End Award Winner, (Best New Musical) and *The Lighthouse* (Production Exchange).

As Composer: *The Twits* (Curve), *The Importance of Being Earnest* (Curve/Birmingham Rep), *The Witches* (Curve/West Yorkshire Playhouse), *Teddy* (Southwark Playhouse – Off West End winner, Best New Musical), *The Snow Queen* (Royal and Derngate/Nuffield), *The Bacchae* and *Blood Wedding* (Royal & Derngate – during the Cameron Mackintosh/Mercury Musicals Resident composer scheme), *The Merchant of Venice*, *Merry Wives of Windsor* and *The Comedy of Errors* (Changeling Theatre) and *Captured by the Dark* (StopGap Theatre).

Songs by Dougal have featured at three WhatsonStage Award winners' concerts and the song cycles *A Song Cycle for Soho* (Soho Theatre) and *Beyond the Gate* (Gate Theatre). His album *Acoustic Overtures: The Songs of Dougal Irvine* features a foreword by Stephen Fry and the 'Stiles and Drewe song prize' winning *Do You Want A Baby Baby?*

Dougal was also a finalist for Anthony Gormley's Arts Foundation Award.

CAST

2018

TEDDY	George Parker
JOSIE	Molly Chesworth
JOHNNY VALENTINE	Dylan Wood
SAMMY 'THE STICKS' SMITH	Andrew Gallo
JENNY O'MALLEY	Freya Parks
BUSTER WATSON	Harrison White

2015

TEDDY	Joseph Prowen
JOSIE	Jennifer Kirby
JOHNNY VALENTINE	Will Payne
SAMMY 'THE STICKS' SMITH	Alexander Bean
JENNY O'MALLEY	Alice Offley
BUSTER WATSON	Harrison White

Creative teams were the same for both shows:

Director – Eleanor Rhode
Musical Director – Harrison White
Choreographer – Tom Jackson Greaves
Set Designer – Max Dorey
Costume Designer – Holly Rose Henshaw
Lighting Designer – Christopher Nairne
Sound Designer – Max Pappenheim

ACKNOWLEDGEMENTS

It took me four years to write *Teddy*: four years of thinking about the idea, letting it rattle around in my head, and then when it came to putting pen to paper, the first draft poured out in just two weeks. After that, it went from first draft to first night in eleven months – which is, quite frankly, an insane speed.

Three years after that, we finally got it out on the road and on tour. It has taken an inordinately large number of people to get *Teddy* to where it is now, and I'd like to thank a few of them for their invaluable help, love and support:

Eleanor Rhode – for being one of the best directors I know.

Sarah Loader – for being one of the best producers I know.

Paul Hart – for enjoying *Teddy* so much he saw it twice (sorry about there being no interval before).

Jim Zalles – for helping to get *Teddy* off the damn ground in the first place.

Every staff member and volunteer at The Vaults, Watermill Theatre, Southwark Playhouse and every other venue where *Teddy* has played – from Production and Marketing to Front of House and Box Office, thank you for your time, help and efforts.

The cast, crew and creative team – for making the show look, sound and feel so goddamn fantastic.

My agent, Katie Langridge – for seeing *Teddy* the first time round and thinking "This chump might have something."

Lucy – there's no one else I'd rather dance through life with.

Mum, Dad, Butts and Bakerloo – for all the music and all the swearing.

T.B.
April 2018

*This play is dedicated to David Brown –
may we all be as lucky to have a teacher as good as him.*

CHARACTERS

TEDDY – a Teddy Boy, eighteen
JOSIE – a Teddy Girl, seventeen
JOHNNY VALENTINE AND THE BROKEN HEARTS – a rock 'n' roll band
JOHNNY VALENTINE – vocals and rhythm guitar
BUSTER WATSON – lead guitar and piano
JENNY O'MALLEY – bass
SAMMY "THE STICKS" SMITH – drums

TIME

1956

SETTING

Elephant and Castle, south London

AUTHOR'S NOTE

... indicates something unsaid.

– indicates an interrupted or unfinished thought.

Side A

Darkness.

JOHNNY VALENTINE *is alone onstage.*

JOHNNY VALENTINE A wise man once said, "Ambition ain't nothin' but a dream with a V8 engine." Well, I been behind the wheel of that dream for a while now – travelin' the world, cuttin' records, playin' the radio – but there ain't no part of it I like better than being in front of a crowd. Face to face, I mean. That's sump'n special. Cos when you just sendin' songs out on the airwaves – you never know who's out there in the darkness. You never know who's listenin'.

He smiles.

Radio static and crackle...then:

SAMMY "THE STICKS" SMITH Good evenin' cool cats and cool kittens, this is Radio Be-Bop and I'm smitten with that tune, that's a fact, ain't no doubt about that. We gettin' geared up for Saturday night and we got tunes to put you and yours in the swingin' mood, so start puttin' on those glad rags, slick back your hair and I'll be back after this next number – don't go anywhere.

SONG: "READY TEDDY"

HAIR SLICKED BACK, IT'S BLACK AND MEAN
I'M THE COOLEST CAT THAT YOU EVER DONE SEEN
COS I'M READY, TEDDY, READY TO GO
READY, TEDDY, READY TO GO
GIVE ME ROCK 'N' ROLL AND NICE, FAST BEAT
COS I'M READY TEDDY
READY TO GO

TEDDY I check myself in the glass one more time.

JOSIE Check my hair.

TEDDY Pulled back and black like an oil slick.

JOSIE Pony tail jutting high, my fringe spilled out like rubble.

TEDDY I run the comb through one more time to get it right, just right. Pomade clings to my fingers, rough and tangy like motor oil.

JOSIE Another spray, a spurt and it's held in place, high and ready like a starter's pistol.

TEDDY I turn to the side. My quiff a crest that peaks high and cuts through the air like a shark's fin.

JOSIE I pout my lips and paint them red, pucker and kiss the mirror and leave behind a scarlet O that looks like a blood-red bullet wound.

TEDDY My skin's a little sore and raw from the cheap razor, but it's smooth enough. It'll have to do for tonight.

JOSIE Bang bang – you're dead.

TEDDY In my bedroom, the record stops…

Music stops.

…and the next one drops.

Music continues.

JOSIE The plastic platter tumbles then crackles static and there's a hush.

TEDDY A little quiver.

JOSIE Anticipation.

TEDDY Then his voice comes in.

JOSIE Big and blue and so fucking lovely.

TEDDY Swirling all the way from the bottom and reaching up to the top.

JOSIE Johnny Valentine.

TEDDY Fuck me.

JOHNNY VALENTINE
> STEP OUT TO MEET MY GIRL SO FINE
> A GAL SO SWEET SHE BLOWS MY MIND
>
> COS I'M READY, TEDDY, READY TO GO
> READY, TEDDY, READY TO GO
> GIVE ME ROCK 'N' ROLL AND NICE, FAST BEAT
> COS I'M READY TEDDY
> READY TO GO

JOSIE Oh my god!

TEDDY That voice!

JOSIE Gets me right here.

TEDDY What a voice!

JOSIE Makes my blood pump and my curls wind tighter.

TEDDY Like he's revving an engine.

JOSIE Makes you wanna move about.

TEDDY People listen to you when you got a voice like that.

JOSIE Barely keep my feet still.

TEDDY You don't even have to make 'em – they just listen!

JOSIE But I pull myself together and pull my clothes on. Sling on my shirt, crisp, white and tight.

TEDDY Drainpipe skinnies that cling to me like a lover, rooted in leopard-skin creepers.

JOSIE Thick rolls in my jeans that show skinny white ankles.

TEDDY My tie a thin black line from neck to navel.

JOSIE Pinched round my throat, a flash of knotted red to match the lips.

TEDDY Wide collar and velvet lapels on a drop-down coat.

JOSIE A man's blazer, battered and bruised black and blue, pinched in the middle with a single brass button.

TEDDY A gun-metal buckle round my midriff.

JOSIE I check myself in the mirror.

TEDDY One last time.

In tempo, music stops.

JOSIE Be honest.

TEDDY *and* **JOSIE** I look fucking good.

JOHNNY VALENTINE
HEAD TO A JOINT THAT'S JUMPIN' WITH JIVE
WE THE MEANEST PAIR OF SWINGERS EVER ALIVE

COS I'M READY, TEDDY, READY TO GO
READY, TEDDY, READY TO GO
GIVE ME ROCK 'N' ROLL AND NICE, FAST BEAT
COS I'M READY TEDDY
READY TO GO

WE ROCK ALL NIGHT, NO NEED FOR BED
SHE'S A STONE-COLD FOX, I'M A MEAN OL' TED

COS I'M READY, TEDDY, READY TO GO
READY, TEDDY, READY TO GO
GIVE ME ROCK 'N' ROLL AND NICE, FAST BEAT
COS I'M READY TEDDY
READY TO GO
READY TEDDY READY TO GO
READY TEDDY READY TO GO

Music dead stop with – doorbell.

JOSIE My reflections are shattered and I'm brought back to the matter in hand, namely: Saturday night.

TEDDY Alright.

JOSIE The bell again, and then I'm straight down the stairs, on the back of my neck the hairs are still stood to attention at the thought so sublime of sweet Johnny Valentine.

TEDDY I nip in the front room.

JOSIE A quick look round for my dad. The coast is clear.

TEDDY I reach for the key from beneath the Bakelite set.

JOSIE I know exactly where the key is kept, then turn the lock on my old man's cabinet. Grab a bottle.

TEDDY Slip a swig.

JOSIE A glug.

TEDDY It burns.

JOSIE Never get used to the taste.

TEDDY But in the bottom of my belly it lights a lovely little fire that gives that glow, you know, that you need for a Saturday night? Gets you kickstarted and feeling just right.

JOSIE The stink of the gin is grassy and oily. I wipe my hands on a doily then make for the door.

Drum punctuation.

A roar from upstairs.

"Is that you, girl?"

Shit. Gotta be quick.

"Where are you off to? Where are you going?"

But right now there's no way of knowing.

Music starts. Guitar.

The night is young and so am I. I got the whole night.

TEDDY The whole world.

JOSIE Unfurled out in front of me, I can do what I like. His roar again, which I again ignore, and instead make a turn quick smart for the door but with hand on the latch I catch something in the corner of my eye, hanging off the back of the kitchen door. My father's work coat. Limp and lonely, hanging condemned till Monday morning comes round again. I should go while the going's good and split. But right now the booze that sits in my belly whispers words to my fingers, which eagerly kitchen-wards twitch.

If I'm careful. If I'm quick.

I slide my hand inside, real gentle like, and see what I can find. Shilling and six. Nothing much. But things being such as they are I ain't one to stare a gift horse in the mouth, 'specially what with my finances heading the way they are – namely south. I turn.

"Didn't you hear me? You fucking deaf or what?"

– he bellows, his booze-soaked breath right in my face –

"Where you going dressed like that?"

– his face a bulldog grimace and stinking drunk –

"You look like a bloke. You look like a dyke."

I'm goin' out.

"And who said you could go anywhere tonight? Did I tell you that you could go out?"

I try to push past, the coin clutched in my fist.

"What you got there, girl?"

Nothing.

"Don't lie to me."

– he growls and grabs my wrist. Get off! You're hurting me.

"Hurtin' ya? I ain't even started yet. You lyin' to me, I'll make you sorry, girl, I swear I fuckin' –"

Doorbell.

TEDDY The front door.

JOSIE But before he can finish I stamp on his foot. He roars, his face contorted in anger, the veins on his brow cable thick but quick I take the money, stuff it deep in my pocket.

TEDDY I glide over smooth as I can.

JOSIE Straight to the door, unlock it, step out on the street where I meet –

TEDDY My boys.

Short stop with bass.

JOSIE My girls.

Short stop with bass.

SONG: "SHAKE, RATTLE AND RAIL"

JENNY
I AIN'T GONNA SPEND THE LONG COLD NIGHTS
SCRUBBIN' YOUR DIRTY FLOORS
I AIN'T GONNA SPEND THE LONG COLD NIGHTS
DOIN' ALL YOUR CHORES
YOU SET ME TO DOIN' HOUSEWORK
I'M GONNA KICK YOU OUT THE DOOR

JENNY *and* **JOHNNY**
ALL WE NEED IS A HOT JUKE BOX AND ICE BOX FULL OF ALE
ALL WE NEED IS A HOT JUKE BOX AND ICE BOX FULL OF ALE
WE AIN'T GONNA SWEEP, WE GONNA STAMP OUR FEET
WE GONNA SHAKE, RATTLE AND RAIL

TEDDY George and Jenners, turned out real nice.

JOSIE Susi and Fran, hand in hand in china doll hats, frock coats and black flats, hair piled high and two pairs of lips dipped in blood-red rouge.

TEDDY Electric-blue frock coat with bolo tie and winklepickers for George, pinstripe three-piece with cream turn-up cuffs and – flashy bastard – diamond-studded tie pin for Jenners. A rock as big as your fist, just there.

JOSIE The girls stop to chat but I can hear my father's footsteps and in two steps I grab the girls and drag them down the street, looking back to see the red-faced ogre howling revenge, "I swear to God I'll kill you if ever step foot in his house again. You hear me? I'll fuckin' kill ya!"

TEDDY We leave the empty house and step into the night.

JOSIE But why the fuck would I wanna ever go back there? I pick up the pair and arm in arm quick sharp we escape any harm as we link up and march out beneath the ink-black sky.

TEDDY Pavement slick with rain.

JOSIE Susi launches a brolly and its wide wings save our hair from disaster and we put a rush on and walk faster.

TEDDY We run down the road, soles slapping the streets to make for the shelter, the sweat-ridden swelter of the bus stop, George screaming all the way and pulling at my tails like a grinning madman.

JOSIE We huddle together and light up a fag, whilst nearby sit two sour old bags who look at us like shit on a shoe.

TEDDY A pair of blue rinsers with barely their dentures still stuck in their gums sit staring at us with looks of disgust as we sit and wait for the bus to come.

JOSIE And as we walk and smoke, Fran cackles and jokes about some sick Smoothie tried to make a pass, grab her arse and ended up with a knee in the balls for his troubles, and through the haze of my fag I see them two ladies still staring, *(Music cuts out)* just staring at us until one says to her mate –

Drums return.

TEDDY "Why they dressed like that? Like a peacock that's gone wrong."

JOSIE "Ladies don't dress like that, or act like that, or smoke like that."

TEDDY "Where they get the money for them clothes?"

JOSIE "They honestly spend their money on a get-up like that?"

TEDDY "On them silly clothes?"

JOSIE "Rent to buy, I suppose. They're all on credit, these kids."

TEDDY "Wouldn't know an honest day's work if it slapped them in the face."

JOSIE "Well they could do with a slap."

TEDDY "A real gent wouldna spent so much which he don't have on such silly shoes like that."

JOSIE Well well.

TEDDY That's lucky, in't it?

JOSIE Cos I ain't a lady.

TEDDY I ain't no gent.

JOSIE "What are you then?"

TEDDY Ain't it obvious? I'm a Ted.

JOSIE Born and bred. Won't ever catch me bein' a lady.

TEDDY I flash 'em a grin and give 'em a wink, they flush and turn pink.

JOSIE I blow a vaporous O, a perfect ring of smoke that hangs in the air like it just came out of the barrel of a gun. Bang bang – you're dead.

TEDDY Feathers ruffled –

JOSIE They cough and splutter.

TEDDY – and mutter and shuffle as the bus pulls up and the three of us mount it.

JOSIE Back of the bus with the bottle passed hand to hand we plan what the night has in store and how it will be spent. And I tell you sump'n for nothin'.

TEDDY Whatever we end up doing.

JOSIE I won't ever end up no lady.

Band smash.

TEDDY And I won't never end up no gent.

Band smash.

JENNY
> YOU WANT YOURSELF A LITTLE MISS?
> YOU OUTTA YOUR DOG-GONE MIND
> YOU WANT YOURSELF A LITTLE MISS?
> BROTHER YOU SURE BE BLIND
> COS I'M A HOT ROD MAMMA MOVIN' SO FAST
> I'M GONNA LEAVE YOU DRAGGIN' BEHIND

JENNY *and* **JOHNNY**
> ALL WE NEED IS A HOT JUKE BOX AND ICE BOX FULL OF ALE
> ALL WE NEED IS A HOT JUKE BOX AND ICE BOX FULL OF ALE
> WE AIN'T GONNA SWEEP, WE GONNA STAMP OUR FEET
> WE GONNA SHAKE, RATTLE AND RAIL

JOSIE The bus comes to a stop and off we all hop.

TEDDY At last, the rain is subsiding but leaving behind these filthy fat, flat puddles like stretched-out steel that cling to the streets for dear life.

JOSIE We make a sharp left and head down an alley, Fran out in front crackling laughter and Susi and I come barrelling after, the sounds of howls bouncing off the walls like buckshot. The bottle is tossed between us and the liquor lingers on my tongue and begins to run further inside to stoke the little fire in my belly, burnin' quite nicely and glowin' so warm.

TEDDY Past Liverpool Grove and Portland Street, two alleyways meet and at the bottom past the rubble and dust there's a rusted chainlink fence peeled back like an unbuttoned shirt, which we clamber through – making sure that our shoes aren't sullied and soiled – and for all our toils we are granted admission to the Church. Two stories of bombed-out nothing, high crumbling walls and a roof that ain't there anymore. It hangs on the backstreets of London like a battered rib cage, empty and wheezing and waiting to die. They keep promisin' to knock it down, do sump'n with it – finish off the job that Adolf didn't – but they never do. And yeah, sure, it ain't much to look at but – for now – it's ours.

JENNY *and* **JOHNNY**
　　ALL WE NEED IS A HOT JUKE BOX AND ICE BOX FULL OF ALE
　　ALL WE NEED IS A HOT JUKE BOX AND ICE BOX FULL OF ALE
　　WE AIN'T GONNA SWEEP, WE GONNA STAMP OUR FEET
　　WE GONNA SHAKE, RATTLE AND RAIL

JOSIE　There's two dozen Teds peacocking their threads and a gaggle of dollies armed with clutch bags and brollies hooked on their arms like sweethearts, laughing and joking with smoke rings that puff from their lips like factory towers.

TEDDY　The party's already underway and guys and girls meet and swirl like a spirit and mixer, all the quicker for the trickle of liquor that flows from hand to hand and lip to lip.

JOSIE　Someone's brought a radio, music up and blastin' from a tinny little thing that threatens to choke from the dust thrown up by the dancing feet.

JENNY
　　I WON'T RATTLE NO PANS, I WON'T CLEAN NO DISHES
　　DADDY-O, YOU JUST TRY
　　I WON'T MOP NO FLOORS OR SCRUB NO SHEETS,
　　DADDY-O, YOU JUST TRY
　　O BOY YOU TRY TO MAKE ME, I'LL BUST YOUR LIP
　　AND SPIT IN YOUR EYE

BAND　*(First time a capella)*
　　ALL WE NEED IS A HOT JUKE BOX AND ICE BOX FULL OF ALE
　　ALL WE NEED IS A HOT JUKE BOX AND ICE BOX FULL OF ALE
　　WE AIN'T GONNA SWEEP, WE GONNA STAMP OUR FEET
　　WE GONNA SHAKE, RATTLE AND RAIL

　　ALL WE NEED IS A HOT JUKE BOX AND ICE BOX FULL OF ALE
　　ALL WE NEED IS A HOT JUKE BOX AND ICE BOX FULL OF ALE
　　WE AIN'T GONNA SWEEP, WE GONNA STAMP OUR FEET
　　WE GONNA SHAKE, RATTLE AND RAIL

Big finish from band.

JOSIE I lean back, fag lit, quietly sit and watch the girls chatter and jaw, the rattling caw of gossiping crows that echoes against the bare brick walls.

TEDDY Plan is to squat there an hour or two, smoke a few, drink and screw around – then what?

JOSIE "The cinema," says Susi.

TEDDY George says the flicks.

JOSIE "See what pics they got up on the big screen."

TEDDY "*Blackboard Jungle*," Jenners says, "Man, I hear that picture's pumping."

JOSIE But I ain't got the money to waste on the flicks.

TEDDY That's the key, innit?

JOSIE The cash –

TEDDY – which like a flash in the pan is here and then gone.

JOSIE I mean that what I took from my dad has already been had on the bus, booze and fags.

TEDDY And now I find my pockets, light on lucre and long overdue for refilling.

JOSIE And so penniless and with options less, I imagine the perfect night in all its dreamy detail.

TEDDY A crawl, pub to pub.

JOSIE Glass to glass, chasing last orders.

TEDDY The Moon and The Swan.

JOSIE The Red Lion, The Flag.

TEDDY The Crown then The Stag.

JOSIE And when the pubs are dry and the drink is done, and the slap of old flat feet on washed-out streets comes to a crescendo, what next?

TEDDY Dancing.

SIDE A

JOSIE Somewhere with music.

TEDDY "Old Joe's," says George, "they got nice birds in there." But fuck that for a game of soldiers. That place is square as they come. Row upon row of fat little frumps with their boyfriends in tow, all pushing at the bar, all elbows and angles. Watching your duds as the ash dangles from the fag-tipped fat lip of some clueless Smoothie in a cheap nylon suit who wants to watch where he puts his fucking cigarette, mate.

JOSIE But it turns out Susi and Fran have got it planned already cos the two of them have been going toe to toe with these two greasy beaus they met in Old Joe's last Saturday night and they've got a friend, see, who heard about me and is dying to make my acquaintance – which I ain't. But when I tell 'em as much they harpy-shriek and their squeaking voices pitch and twist over each other and grate in my ears till it's clear that they won't take no for an answer and so I succumb. "Okay," I say, "I'll come!" I don't really care where we go, what we do, as long as they got Johnny fuckin' Valentine playin' all night long.

JOHNNY VALENTINE Now listen up guys and girls, and you'd better listen up quick.

TEDDY What was that?

JOHNNY VALENTINE Now I ain't one to go tellin' tall tales.

TEDDY The radio – turn it up!

JOHNNY VALENTINE But I think you're gonna wanna hear this.

TEDDY Listen!

JOHNNY VALENTINE Cos after my sold-out show at the Trocadero tonight I'm gonna be playing a secret set at a groovy little hideaway called Teddy's. With such a VIP present, admission ain't cheap – but if you can hustle the cash, dash yourself down there tonight for a show that you ain't never gonna forget. But this is a secret gig, you dig? I'm only tellin' you all this cos I like you so much. So keep it on the down-low, stay tuned and I hope I'll be seein' you at the show.

Music. Guitar harmonics evolving to love theme.

TEDDY The effect is immediate, immense, every single mind turned tense and taught with the thought of standing within arm's length of that silver-voiced Adonis, almost able to touch him. The thought is almost blasphemy – but as for me, at that very moment my thoughts are elsewhere entwined cos through the sinuous crowd, between the quiffs and the curls, I notice a girl, sat back in repose and real proud like, a knowing smile drawn on her lips as she watches the rest of the Judies and sips at a bottle. Not saying nothing – just looking and watching – and she's still. Real still.

JOSIE They're tellin' me about this fella – Tully, he's called, sleek, slick, suave and flush with cash, keen to flash it and show us a good Saturday night and – yeah alright, I ain't that thrilled about the prospect but seeing as I've no cash or plan and it ain't like I can go home any time soon, what choice have I got? But while the girls keep on prattlin', their tongues all a-rattlin' I just sit and listen – well not really listen cos I find that in such situations if I sit real still, people will just carry on with a roar and a rush, and in your own little hush you sit silent for a moment, watch the world pass a million miles an hour and just –

TEDDY Got a light?

JOSIE What?

TEDDY I said got a light?

JOSIE For what?

TEDDY What d'you think? For a fag.

JOSIE No – I ain't.

TEDDY Well then give us a drag. I ain't see you before.

JOSIE Well I ain't seen you neither.

TEDDY Down here all the time. Most Saturdays at least – better than hanging out in the streets.

JOSIE Why's that?

TEDDY People think we're trouble.

JOSIE Maybe you are.

TEDDY You sound like my old lady.

JOSIE Your old lady sounds like me.

TEDDY I'm Teddy.

JOSIE Are you?

TEDDY By name and by nature.

JOSIE What – you mean all stuffed and cuddly?

TEDDY I'm serious.

JOSIE So am I.

TEDDY No you ain't. I seen you smile.

JOSIE I don't smile.

TEDDY Tell that to those lips.

JOSIE I'll tell it to yours with my fucking fist.

TEDDY Easy, easy – I'm only playing.

JOSIE And he flashes me a smile. Disarming and charming, a little alarming, and despite my best efforts the fires in my belly are stoked – just a little, for a moment – there's a glow and I feel –

"Who the fuck is this chump?"

– says a voice thick and lump as clay from behind me. I turn and there's a six-foot gorilla squeezed in a suit, meaty hands metallic with golden rings and with two underlings that hang about him like little boys eager to please. This must be Tully. A thick-lipped bruiser with a face like a cracked tin of Spam.

"You chattin' to my chickadee, chum?"

I ain't your chickadee, Tully, and chattin' ain't illegal.

"The girl's with me, you see?"

– he says, ignoring me outright and setting his gaze right at the Smiler who's stood next to me –

"So buzz off, short stuff – go back to the playground."

TEDDY You go back to the jungle.

JOSIE "You what?"

TEDDY You heard.

JOSIE "Fuck me – baby boy's got a big mouth. Hope he's got big fists too."

TEDDY And he jabs a fat finger in my chest, and I jab it right back. He grabs my lapel and I grab his and from his pocket I see a black handle, hear a click and a flick of sharp silver and it looks like blood might fall before night does until –

JOSIE Oi – stop it! Like a couple of fucking kids, you are. You supposed to be showing me a good night, in't ya? You wanna start with a fight or what?

"Alright darlin', go easy on ol' Tully,"

– he leers with lip-curled grin, before turnin' to Smiler and sayin' –

"Next time, fella,"

– before his fingers slowly unwind and he lollops away, knuckles in the dirt and while nobody's hurt, I can tell he's bruised his pride.

TEDDY Thanks.

JOSIE For what?

TEDDY For helpin' me out.

JOSIE I just don't like to see an idiot get hurt.

TEDDY Oh, I wouldna hurt him too bad.

JOSIE I'm glad about that. Well – it's been real.

TEDDY You goin'?

JOSIE Looks like it.

TEDDY Where?

JOSIE What's it to you?

TEDDY Just curious.

JOSIE Pictures.

TEDDY You never told me your name.

JOSIE No, I didn't.

TEDDY See you around then?

JOSIE Maybe.

TEDDY And with that she's off, turns and trots towards her two other Judies that dangle from her arms like bracelet charms, with the gorilla and his two chimps in tow showin' just a bit too much interest for my likin'. But that don't matter a bit cos if I was a bettin' man – which I'm not, cos I ain't got two shillings to rub together – but if I was I'd bet myself whether or not that, even though she's playin' it cool, that was a smile that just passed those lips, directed my way, curled up for an instant then dipped before anyone could notice – but meant expressly for me.

"Who was that?" says George at my side.

No idea.

"Nevermind," Jenners says, "so – we doin' sump'n or what?"

Sure. Let's see what's on at the pictures.

"Thought you didn't wanna go to the flicks?"

Ain't a man allowed to change his mind?

JOHNNY VALENTINE Folks, I figure I should take a moment to introduce you to this here band o' mine: the Broken Hearts. This here's Buster Watson. He don't say much. Lets his guitar do most of the talkin'. Ain't that right, Bus'?

A flourish or solo from **BUSTER.**

That there fella on the drums is Sammy "The Sticks" Smith. How we doin', Sammy?

SAMMY "THE STICKS" SMITH Oh we cookin' wit' gas, Johnny, we cookin' wit' gas.

JOHNNY VALENTINE Sammy: why they call you "The Sticks"?

A short and blistering solo from **SAMMY.**

SAMMY "THE STICKS" SMITH That answer your question?

JOHNNY VALENTINE And that sweet lady slappin' the bass is Jenny O'Malley.

Sexy bass lick from **JENNY.**

How you doin' tonight, Jen?

JENNY O'MALLEY I'm doin' just fine, Johnny.

JOHNNY VALENTINE You lookin' mighty purty. Jenny here brings a feminine touch to the group.

JENNY O'MALLEY You wanna feel my feminine touch clean across any of your jaws?

JOHNNY VALENTINE Hell no – it's tough being a lady in this business.

JENNY O'MALLEY Honey, real rock 'n' roll is about heartache, sufferin' and pain. If that ain't a woman's business, I don't know what is.

JOHNNY VALENTINE Well, speakin' 'bout heartache, sufferin' and pain, we got another love song for you – all about the girl of our dreams. And if you gonna dream, you best dream big.

SONG: "A GAL FROM HOLLYWOOD"
SOME FOLKS ARE ALRIGHT ON A SATURDAY NIGHT
OUT DANCING WITH THEIR CHICKS
BUT NOT ME, NO SIR, I GIVE YOU MY WORD I'M IN MUCH
   MORE OF A FIX

COS MY GAL, SHE'S SWEET, SUCH A HOT-LIPPED TREAT
WHO KNOWS HOW TO GET HER KICKS
BUT THE ONLY TIME I SEE A GAL SO FINE
IS WHEN I GO TO THE PICS

JOHNNY VALENTINE	BAND
I'M IN LOVE WITH A GAL FROM HOLLYWOOD	LOVE LOVE LOVE WITH A GAL FROM, A GAL FROM HOLLYWOOD
I'M IN LOVE WITH A GAL FROM HOLLYWOOD	LOVE LOVE LOVE WITH A GAL FROM, A GAL FROM HOLLYWOOD

JOHNNY VALENTINE

I'M IN LOVE WITH A MOVIE STARLET
AND YOU KNOW THAT AIN'T NO GOOD

I'M GONNA SEE MY BLUE-EYED BABY
UP THERE ON THE SILVER SCREEN
FORTY-FOOT HIGH, SHE MAKES ME DIE
AND HAUNTS ALL OF OUR DREAMS
I'M A LOVE SICK FOOL, I'M A-FAILING SCHOOL
AND MY WALLET'S EMPTY AND LEAN
COS I SPEND EVERY DIME WAITING IN LINE
JUST TO WATCH HER ON THAT SCREEN

JOHNNY VALENTINE	BAND
I'M IN LOVE WITH A GAL FROM HOLLYWOOD	LOVE LOVE LOVE WITH A GAL FROM, A GAL FROM HOLLYWOOD
I'M IN LOVE WITH A GAL FROM HOLLYWOOD	LOVE LOVE LOVE WITH A GAL FROM, A GAL FROM HOLLYWOOD

JOHNNY VALENTINE

I'M IN LOVE WITH A MOVIE STARLET
AND YOU KNOW THAT AIN'T NO GOOD

Repeat chorus.

End of song. Drum and bass continue.

JOSIE The queue outside the Coronet is immense.

TEDDY Half the Teds in London must be here tonight.

JOSIE But we manage to make it in.

TEDDY No problem.

JOSIE Tully simply marches past bold as brass all the queuing crowds who – given Tully's height (monstrous) and his face (grotesque) – think it best not to complain.

TEDDY VIP entrance. I say entrance – lav window, but you know beggars can't be choosers and as the last of our trio slides through the glass we begin to make our way past the ushers and ascend to the dark of the gallery where we can see the whole place is jumping.

Guitar interlude.

JOSIE The feature ain't started but the party's already in full swing: bottles passed row to row, fags aglow as their tips light the air like stars, Teds draped at all angles over red velvet seats, their brothel-creeper feet dangling and lazily swinging.

TEDDY Back row couples comingle – I can feel the air tingle as the guys and their girls are wound closely and swirled into each other – Slow down, pet! We ain't even past the trailers, don't tire him out yet!

JOSIE Tully's two lackeys, name of Derek and Snitch (no idea which is which), have wrangled six seats from a terrified group of kids and so we all sit – Susi and Fran each with an interchangeable man and myself sat shoulder to shoulder with Tully.

Music softens.

He offers up his popcorn which I politely scorn and seemingly unfazed he fills his gob with it and chews it cow-like and now, like some lothario, offers me another greasy wink.

"You like the flicks?"

'S alright.

"I love 'em, me. Come here every week – twice sometimes. Sci-fi, westerns and what-not – I love all that. Tell you what – you could be in the movies, couldn't ya? You ever wanted to be in the movies?"

Ain't never really thought about it.

"Course you have – all girls wanna be in the movies. Goodlookin' girl like you, you're dynamite. Born movie starlet, in't ya?"

– he whispers in my ear, his breath a rank combo of popcorn, fags and beer. I shrug his compliments, turn to Fran and Susi for help but see they are otherwise involved, lip to lip with their two gormless chimps, and so abandoned and stranded with this gorilla see no option else but to grit my teeth, ignore his lecherous leering and screen-ward fix my face, and pray it's a short movie.

Full band continues.

TEDDY I look for the girl 'mongst the jittering rows, but who knows where she could be? There's so many here, and it's clear the crowd is getting restless, bubblin' and threatenin' to boil over less somethin' happens soon but then –

Band silence.

JOSIE – with a click –

TEDDY – and a snap –

JOSIE – everything goes black.

TEDDY And above our heads –

JOSIE – a tunnel of silver pulses and threads –

TEDDY – widens and spreads against the screen.

JOSIE A thousand eyes widen, gazing transfixed as black and white mix to make the image before us, and just like that –

TEDDY – in an instant –

JOSIE – we're there.

TEDDY New York City. The rough side.

JOSIE Looks a lot like here.

TEDDY A classroom.

JOSIE A teacher.

TEDDY Buzzcut, cheap suit, rod up his arse at the front of the class preaching some lesson or other. Suddenly a dirty word is spoke, a joke at his expense that ripples the classroom in laughter and the teacher looks direct at the culprit and says –

"What was that?"

JOSIE "You heard,"

– says its speaker, a brooding dark-haired cat sleeker, slicker and quicker in thought and word than the buzzcut bozo by the blackboard.

TEDDY "Say that again."

JOSIE "Why – you deaf, grandpa?"

TEDDY "Okay. That's it. You're going to the principal's office. Now."

JOSIE "Am I?"

TEDDY "You bet, now I'm tellin' you – get, you little punk, get!"

JOSIE "You're tellin' me? Tellin' me, tellin' me, you always tellin' me. Well now I'm tellin' you sump'n. You want me to go, you better make me. You gonna make me – daddy-o?"

TEDDY And then simple and quick from his hand comes a flick and a blade, long and sharp, darts from between his digits and dazzles in the light.

JOSIE I gasp and lean in, so gripped I barely care or notice that Tully has slid an anaconda arm around my shoulders. I can smell the BO and his stench, and ordinarily I would flatten his nose but right now I don't care – I can't wrench my eyes from the movie.

TEDDY "You feelin' groovy, daddy-o? You wanna dance?"

JOSIE His hand slides on my knee, I brush it aside.

TEDDY "Cos I got a partner for you right here."

JOSIE He makes a move again but I shrug him off, lean right in, my eyes open wide, close to the screen as I can, close to the action.

TEDDY "You know, for a bright boy you ain't that smart."

JOSIE "Where you want this blade?"

TEDDY "In the belly?"

JOSIE "In the heart?"

TEDDY Then all of a sudden –

Drum roll, drums underscore following section.

JOSIE – he's on him! They wrestle and scuff and the crowd on screen and off bellow and jeer, boo Buzzcut and cheer Our Hero on in the fight.

TEDDY Then a crowning blow!

JOSIE Our hero's fist connects with jaw, Buzzcut buckles and falls to the floor –

Music stops.

– a moment of pause, the crowd is left silent in shock and then – bang!

TEDDY Forty-foot letters burst onto the screen, the title: *Blackboard Jungle*.

JOSIE And then an onslaught and rush as the uncertain hush is shattered by the boom of Bill Hayley.

We hear the opening lines of "ROCK AROUND THE CLOCK" by Bill Hayley.*

Band continues in surreal style of music.

JOSIE And the cinema erupts!

TEDDY A roar from the guts of each and every one of us bursts outward and up and spreads from our throats to our feet.

JOSIE And as we leap from our seats, the music so sweet and jumpin' it's makin' the blood pump in our veins and with no restrain, like a horse without reins, the crowd goes completely insane.

TEDDY Heads boppin', knees shakin', bodies movin' so fast they're breakin' laws!

JOSIE Chairs are shattered.

TEDDY Velvet slashed

JOSIE Bottles flung.

TEDDY Glass smashed.

JOSIE The screen is beset and torn to shreds, the tatters flutter and fall like hot ash.

TEDDY And far below I sudden see amongst the quivering bodies a girl movin' about, all clenched fists and kicks and then it suddenly clicks – it's her! From the Church, that's her alright – the one with the smile, though it's hard to tell, moving as she is like 50,000 volts in skinny jeans with pale white ankles, bullet-fast and mean and completely mesmerising.

JOSIE My body shakes like an engine, my heart races fast, I'm revving at a million miles an hour but just then all of a sudden a hand round my hip, a tug at my waist – I turn and in my face is Tully, his thick fingers and fat face attempting to sully this moment.

---

* A licence to produce *Teddy* does not include a performance licence for "ROCK AROUND THE CLOCK". For further information, please see Music Use Note on page v.

"Come here, darlin'," he says, "I wanna dance."

But I throw him off and jump back into the throng, the song, cos you ain't dancing with me, mate, not a fucking chance. But this would-be dancer just don't know how to take no for an answer and fixes my wrist in a vice-like grip and drags me back round, screams in my face –

"Didn't you hear me, you stupid bitch? I wanna fucking dance! You deaf or what?"

Fuck off! I scream, pull back and swing, my knuckles sing as they collide with his nose, which cymbal-crunches and his whole body hunches back and tumbles, his fingers fumbling for grip but he trips and sprawls back on the floor, his jacket ripped, his shirt incarnadine and I feel drunk, elated – like my blood's turned into wine.

TEDDY Fuck me! Did you see that? She laid the bastard cold out flat!

JOSIE I turn –

TEDDY She looks this way.

JOSIE Look up towards the balcony and what should I see but him. The boy from the Church with the smile that set my belly alight starin' back at me – blazin' like a spotlight.

TEDDY We fix each other's gaze across the gap of broken bottles, screaming lungs and full throttle chaos –

JOSIE – which fades away as we are fixed on each other's faces.

TEDDY And I can see that she is –

JOSIE That he is –

TEDDY *and* **JOSIE** – smiling.

Chase music A.

JOSIE Then all of a sudden I feel a pull at my collar – I scream and I holler as I turn and find some red-faced rozzer –

TEDDY Somebody called the pigs!

JOSIE   – pull me off of my feet and drag me kicking and screaming out into the street.

TEDDY   I'm off in pursuit, down the stairs and out front where outside a barrage of bobbies is draggin' out kids one by one and slingin' them in the backs of their vans. I push through the panic, swim 'gainst the current, till all of a sudden I see that smilin' face (though it's hard to smile with a copper's boot in your back) and I reach out and grab her would-be jailer and in a moment of madness or failure to come up with a better idea, I crack him 'cross the jaw and he yells, turns limp and falls to the floor.

JOSIE   I fall and gasp, look up and see clasping his fingers in a fist the boy from before.

TEDDY   Fuck me – that hurt! It don't look like it hurt that much in the movies.

JOSIE   Look out!

TEDDY   She screams as another copper makes a lunge. I duck, swerve, he misses and plunges face first to concrete and when I try to stop and thank her she screams –

Music cuts out.

JOSIE   Move your arse, leave the wanker!

Chase music B.

They flee. Their escape is wild and frantic, messy and breathless, JOSIE *leading the way and* TEDDY *tumbling after until they finally come to rest in an alley. Hearts pounding, chests heaving,* TEDDY *looks like he might fall over any minute but he regains his composure and his cool before he says –*

TEDDY   I think we lost 'em.

JOSIE   What?

TEDDY I think we lost 'em. The coppers, I mean. I know they're keen but I don't reckon no flatfoot's gonna hot-foot it after us, so no fuss, we're –

Thanks for that back there. Helpin' me. With him. 'Fore he –

You're welcome.

JOSIE What?

TEDDY I said you're welcome.

JOSIE Why – what d'you do?

TEDDY Helped you, that's what. With the copper. Proper decked him I did. Nearly broke my hand.

JOSIE 'S cos you can't punch proper.

TEDDY I know how to fucking fight.

JOSIE Well then how come your hand hurts?

TEDDY Cos he had a tough jaw, alright?

JOSIE Looked pretty flabby to me.

TEDDY I didn't have to help. I coulda left.

JOSIE I can look after myself.

TEDDY Yeah I saw that an' all. That big gorilla you knocked out flat. Saw you do that and I thought, "Fuck me – she can throw a punch." Didn't expect that.

JOSIE What you mean?

TEDDY Well – you know – you bein' a –

JOSIE What – you reckon just cos I got hips and lips, I dunno know how to make a fist?

TEDDY I didn't say that.

JOSIE What you sayin' then?

TEDDY Nothin'.

JOSIE Good.

TEDDY Who was he?

JOSIE Why you wanna know?

TEDDY Don't matter. Just chatter, is all.

JOSIE He was no one.

TEDDY Fucking big no one.

JOSIE Just some fella who couldn't keep his hands to himself.

TEDDY That why you hit him?

JOSIE That's right.

TEDDY Where d'you learn to punch like that?

JOSIE Girl guides.

TEDDY Well – dunno where I'm goin' now. What I'm gonna do rest of the night. What about you?

JOSIE Why you askin'?

TEDDY It's – no, it's nothin'.

JOSIE Don't "No, nothin'." What?

TEDDY There's this club. Teddy's.

JOSIE What they got there?

TEDDY Sump'n special.

JOSIE What – music?

TEDDY A whole lot better.

JOSIE Don't go playin' Mr Mystery.

TEDDY You ain't gonna believe me.

JOSIE Spit it out!

TEDDY Johnny Valentine.

JOSIE ...
    What?

TEDDY Johnny Valentine. Tonight. He's playin' at –

JOSIE Fuck off.

TEDDY What?

JOSIE You're lyin'.

TEDDY I swear I'm not!

JOSIE Johnny Valentine?

TEDDY In the flesh. Everyone's tryna keep it hush-hush, but he's goin' there after the Troc – playin' secret.

JOSIE Oh my God!

TEDDY You like Johnny Valentine?

JOSIE Are you kidding, I – I – Johnny Valentine!

TEDDY I know!

JOSIE He – he's – he's just – just – oh my God!

TEDDY His voice, man, his voice, it's just –

JOSIE It's like a bomb went off.

TEDDY Atomic.

JOSIE Out of sight!

TEDDY Makes you feel –

JOSIE Electric.

TEDDY Goosebumps.

JOSIE Tingles.

TEDDY All the way from the tips of your toes to the top of your quiff.

JOSIE There ain't no one better.

TEDDY People gonna pay to hear me sing like that someday.

JOSIE You?

TEDDY They gonna line the streets to see me sing – here to the horizon – just for a glimpse of my golden notes.

JOSIE Who's gonna listen to you?

TEDDY Everybody. When I sing, I'm gonna make those stars fall out of the sky with sighing, turn the moon to the sun and the sun to the moon. The birds themselves are gonna blush and hush in reverence when I commence to croon.

JOSIE So when can we hear this voice?

TEDDY What?

JOSIE This siren song?

TEDDY Well – I ain't started yet.

JOSIE What?

TEDDY I gotta practise first. Practice makes perfect – and I ain't nothin' if not perfect. You're lookin' at the next Johnny Valentine.

JOSIE You ain't Johnny Valentine. You're a just a two-bit, four-bar nobody.

TEDDY Johnny Valentine was just some nobody once. And everybody's gotta be a nobody before they become a somebody. I'm gonna be the next big thing.

JOSIE The next big thing don't come from a place like this.

TEDDY Well I'm gonna be the first.

JOSIE Dream on.

TEDDY ...
Right.

  TEDDY *goes up the* **BAND**.

  Hey, 'scuse me – hi – yeah, can I get a D?

BUSTER WATSON You what?

TEDDY A D – on the guitar, can I get a –

SIDE A

SONG: "*SHAKE YOU UP*"

BUSTER *plays* **TEDDY** *the chord.*

LISTEN UP, BABY – I AIN'T TELLIN' NO LIES
I AIN'T LIKE NONE O' THEM OTHER GUYS

JENNY *and* **SAMMY** *enter during the song.*

OH WHEN YOU HEAR ME ROCKIN' YOU WON'T SIT STILL
AND IF YOU DON'T WANNA GROOVE THEN YOUR FEET SURE WILL
DON'T RESIST LITTLE MOMMA, YOU'D BETTER GIVE UP
I'M GONNA SHAKE-A SHAKE-A SHAKE-A SHAKE-A SHAKE-A YOU UP

YOUR TOES WILL START A TAPPIN' AND FINGERS START TO TWITCH
SOON YOU'LL START A MOVIN' LIKE YOU'VE GOT A CRAZY ITCH
COS YOU CAUGHT A JITTER BUG AND THERE AIN'T NOTHIN' YOU CAN DO
SOON MY MUSIC'S GONNA TAKE-A TAKE-A TAKE-A YOU

TEDDY	**BAND**
I'M GONNA SHAKE-A SHAKE-A SHAKE-A SHAKE-A SHAKE-A YOU UP	SHAKE-A SHAKE-A SHAKE-A SHAKE-A SHAKE-A YOU UP
SHAKE-A SHAKE-A SHAKE-A SHAKE-A SHAKE-A YOU UP	SHAKE-A SHAKE-A SHAKE-A SHAKE-A SHAKE-A YOU UP

TEDDY

FROM YOUR FINGER TIPS TO YOUR SWINGIN' HIPS
I'M GONNA SHAKE-A SHAKE-A SHAKE-A SHAKE-A SHAKE-A YOU UP!

…

…

…

So.

What you reckon?

JOSIE ...

I –

I –

TEDDY You're smiling.

JOSIE Am I?

TEDDY ...

JOSIE So come on, Hot Shot – what else you got?

TEDDY Pick a tune.

JOSIE Anything?

TEDDY Lady's choice.

JOSIE Charm and a voice. Is there anything you lack?

TEDDY Just try me.

JOSIE "Cool Cadillac".

TEDDY
> OH SHE'S A HUNDRED MILES AN HOUR, RED AND GREEN
> SWEETEST LITTLE MOVER YOU EVER DONE SEEN
> CHERRY RED PAINT WITH LEATHER IN BLACK
> EVERYONE GONNA STARE AT MY COOL CADILLAC

JOSIE "Maggie May!"

TEDDY
> OH MAGGIE MAY, MAGGIE MAY
> PA-PA-PA PLEASE DON'T LEAVE ME THIS WAY
> DON'T LEAVE ME BROKEN-HEARTED, LONELY AND BLUE

JOSIE "Switchblade Sue?"

TEDDY
> I GOT ME A GAL THAT'S TALL AND MEAN
> SHE BREAKS MORE HEARTS THAN A WRECKIN' MACHINE
> SHE CUT YOU OPEN, THAT'S WHAT SHE'LL DO
> THAT'S WHY BOYS CALL HER – SWITCHBLADE SUE

Big finish from the band.

JOSIE You got a pair of pipes on you.

TEDDY I told you. I got quavers to send you a-quiver and arpeggios to make you go weak at the knees. The world ain't gonna know what hit it. Out front. Onstage. Millions of fans. Guys goin' wild and girls goin' wilder.

JOSIE Shoutin' themselves hoarse?

TEDDY Of course.

JOSIE Screamin' your name.

TEDDY Our name.

JOSIE What?

TEDDY Well, I'm gonna need a band, in't I? What you reckon? Way you handled ol' monkey boy back there, you oughta be dynamite on the drums.

JOSIE I don't –

TEDDY Knock a few shades of shit out of the old kit.

JOSIE I don't know how to –

TEDDY Don't matter, you'll learn.

JOSIE I'm not –

TEDDY Or bass, you'd be ace. Slappin' them strings –

JOSIE Shut up.

TEDDY What?

JOSIE I don't sing, I don't play, I don't go daydreamin' about shit that ain't.

TEDDY What's wrong with dreamin'?

JOSIE Wakin' up.

TEDDY What you scared of?

JOSIE What?

TEDDY You heard.

JOSIE I ain't scared.

TEDDY That a fact?

JOSIE I ain't scared of nothin'.

TEDDY Then what's wrong with –

JOSIE Cos it's fuckin' stupid, is all.

TEDDY No more fuckin' stupid than sittin' here waitin' for fuck all to happen. You only get one shot at this life – you wanna waste it stickin' around this shithole forever? The world's bigger than the Walworth Road. I mean – you could go somewhere, do somethin'.

JOSIE Like what?

TEDDY I dunno – whatever you want. Do what you want, when you like. No one tellin' you what to do. *"Tellin' me, tellin' me, you always tellin' me."*

JOSIE What?

TEDDY Like in the movie. The teacher, he's – *"I'm tellin' you – get, you little punk, get."* And the kid is like – *"You're tellin' me? Tellin' me, tellin' me, you always tellin' me."* And he pulls that blade. *"Well now I'm tellin' you sump'n. You want me to go, you better make me. You gonna make me – daddy-o?"*

JOSIE *"You feelin' groovy, daddy-o?"*

TEDDY And then boom!

JOSIE Square in the jaw.

TEDDY Out on the floor.

JOSIE Out like a fucking light.

TEDDY Goodnight.

JOSIE No one's tellin' him what to do. He's doin' whatever he wants.

TEDDY So can we. We can do whatever the fuck we want. What do you wanna do?

JOSIE I – I – I dunno.

TEDDY Come on – anything!

JOSIE Well, what about you?

TEDDY I told you, girl – I'm the next big thing! My voice is gonna sing 'cross the airwaves and whole armies are going march to my door, cryin', beggin', pleadin' for more.

JOSIE I wanna go somewhere. Leave the rubble and dust, the grime and the rust, and dip my feet in the cool blue ocean. California. I seen pictures in a magazine. The sky so wide, the sea a sparklin' green – I'm gonna fly there on a plane – I ain't ever been on one before – head straight for the shore and when I get there I'm gonna get me a brand-new Cadillac. Convertible. Six-cylinder engine. Cherry-red paintwork. Chrome wingtip lights and black leather interior. Gonna drive me up and down the coast, the sun in my hair, the breeze on my lips and with each sip of ocean I'll wash away this shithole clean from memory.

TEDDY We'll go together. You and me.

JOSIE Yeah?

TEDDY What, you think I'm only gonna be big here? They gonna go wild for me over there!

JOSIE After your shows we'll go surfing, then sit on the beach and watch the sun set into the Pacific until nothin' but a quiff, a lick of burning umber that burns the horizon a dusky peachy blue. Not a single fucker there tellin' us what to do.

TEDDY From now on, we gonna do whatever we want.

JOSIE Whatever we like.

TEDDY Startin' tonight.

JOSIE You know what I wanna do? Right now?

TEDDY What?

JOSIE I wanna go see Johnny Valentine.

TEDDY Then let's do it! Why we wastin' time talkin' when we could be waitin' in line for Johnny Valentine? Let's do it!

JOSIE Let's go!

TEDDY What you got?

JOSIE What?

TEDDY Cash. What you got?

JOSIE For what?

TEDDY Teddy's.

JOSIE You gotta pay?

TEDDY How else you think we was gonna get in?

JOSIE I thought you had some.

TEDDY I ain't got none.

JOSIE Well what the fuck we s'posed to do about that?

TEDDY I dunno.

JOSIE Walk up nicely and ask to be let in?

TEDDY I'm thinking!

JOSIE Fuck me.

TEDDY I don't see you comin' up with any ideas.

JOSIE Why don't we just take it?

TEDDY What you mean "take it"? From who?

JOSIE Anyone. Don't matter.

TEDDY What if they don't wanna give it?

JOSIE You tell 'em to give it.

TEDDY What if they don't listen?

JOSIE Then you make 'em listen.

TEDDY But –

JOSIE You scared or sump'n?

TEDDY No.

JOSIE You chicken shit?

TEDDY Fuck no.

JOSIE Then where'd your guts go, boy? Where's your fists? You wanna see Johnny Valentine, yeah? Well we need cash. You think someone's gonna give you that money? You think anyone's just gonna let you sing? Be the next Big Thing? Fortune ain't given, it's taken. You want someone to listen, you make 'em. You want sump'n, you take it. You wanna make it happen, you make it. It's your life.

TEDDY I know.

JOSIE So are you gonna take it?

TEDDY I – I –

JOSIE Are you gonna take it?

TEDDY Yeah – yeah I'm gonna take it!

JOSIE Then do it. Grab it by the throat and don't let go. You only got one shot at this life.

TEDDY One shot?

JOSIE Don't fuckin' miss. So – you with me on this? You gonna take your shot?

TEDDY Where are we?

JOSIE What?

TEDDY What street are we in?

JOSIE Why the fuck you wanna –

TEDDY Quickly, just – tell me: what street we in?

JOSIE I dunno. Says – Coopers Alley or sump'n.

TEDDY 'S only a few streets away.

JOSIE What?

TEDDY I'll be back in a minute.

JOSIE Where you goin'?

TEDDY My house. I gotta get sump'n.

JOSIE What?

TEDDY Our one shot.

TEDDY *runs off and* **JOSIE**'s *left smiling and smoking.*

JOHNNY VALENTINE Well well well, it sure is swell out tonight, ain't it? Stars up there as big as diamonds. There gotta be enough up there for all of us to make a wish on – just make sure you don't go pickin' the wrong star. You don't wanna end up gettin' the wrong wish, do ya? We got a lil' sump'n now, a little slower number for all you stargazers out there – so turn up the volume, pick your star and make yourselves a wish.

Music.

TEDDY Quiet as I can, I turn the handle, which silent-sighs and I inward creep through my front door. I pad 'cross the floor through the gloom, and from the front room I can hear a crackle of tinny voices. I crack the door and sure enough I see my mother, curled up in a ball on the settee, asleep and barely breathing as the radio fills the room with empty voices. Her skin is white, her hair seems whiter, her little fists are tightly balled in fright of everyone and everything and in the sullen dusk she looks like nothing. Nothing but an empty husk.

I turn the dial and with a click the voices die and nothing remains but the noise of an empty house, so vacant that even the echoes have left. I mount the stairs to her room and in the gloom of the back of the closet, I find a metal box – my father's name thereon in cracked, black font – and from beneath the tattered letters, dirty postcards, shabby fetters of wrinkled photos and unwound one-armed watches,

I lift an oily rag, heavy and sagging with its load. A noise downstairs.

"Teddy? Teddy? Is that you?"

I pocket the packet and creep downstairs.

"Teddy?"

– it moans again and I press against the wall before what's left of my mother floats down the hall and up the stairs and I myself slide out the back into the black outside and then a hasty retreat to the alley where I find her sat, fag in fingertips and smoke rising from lips upwards tilted in a lilting smile.

Music stops.

JOSIE You been a while.

TEDDY Nah.

JOSIE Ages.

TEDDY No time at all.

JOSIE So what you rush off for?

He pulls out an old rag and unwraps it. Inside is a gun.

TEDDY You said we should make 'em listen, yeah? Well if they ain't gonna listen to us, maybe they listen to this.

JOSIE ...

Where d'you get that?

TEDDY Dad left it. Got it off a German in the War.

JOSIE You kidding.

TEDDY Took it off him after he killed him. Little memento.

JOSIE Fuck off.

TEDDY You callin' me a liar?

JOSIE Give it here.

TEDDY What?

JOSIE I wanna look at it.

TEDDY No way.

JOSIE Why not?

TEDDY Cos.

JOSIE Cos what?

TEDDY Cos you don't believe me.

JOSIE I do.

TEDDY You don't.

JOSIE I do.

TEDDY You just sayin'.

JOSIE I ain't, I swear. Let me look.

TEDDY Alright.

He passes her the gun.

What you reckon?

She lifts it and looks down the barrel.

JOSIE How many people you reckon it's killed?

TEDDY I dunno.

JOSIE Maybe loads.

TEDDY Maybe.

JOSIE Maybe more.

TEDDY Looks good.

JOSIE You what?

TEDDY You look good. Like an outlaw. Quick draw. Fastest gun in the West.

JOSIE That's cos I am. I'm the very best.

TEDDY What do they call you, gunslinger?

SIDE A   41

JOSIE Josie, if you're my friend – otherwise it's "ma'am". You hear?

TEDDY Loud and clear.

JOSIE Loud and clear what?

TEDDY Loud and clear, ma'am.

JOSIE Damn straight and you keep it that way 'less you wanna be lyin' face first in the dirt.

TEDDY You be careful. There's a gunslinger here gonna test your mettle.

JOSIE Who?

TEDDY Me.

JOSIE You?

TEDDY They call me Lightning Luke. Dead shot every time.

JOSIE That so?

TEDDY I ain't no fluke – when I draw the bullets sing and swim through the air like birds. That gun o' mine's claimed more lives than I can count.

JOSIE Yeah?

She points the pistol at him.

You reckon it's got room for one more?

TEDDY ...

Don't.

JOSIE Stick 'em up.

TEDDY Shut up.

JOSIE I said stick 'em up.

TEDDY I ain't playin'.

JOSIE Me neither.

TEDDY Or what?

JOSIE You know what.

TEDDY It won't work. That thing is old – ancient – ain't meant for shootin', just showin'. Use it to scare 'em, who we rob, do the job better than a knife or a fist – with this people gonna pay attention. It don't work.

JOSIE How d'you know if you don't try?

TEDDY Cos I know is all.

JOSIE You're scared.

TEDDY What?

JOSIE You're scared.

TEDDY I ain't scared.

JOSIE Prove it then.

TEDDY Alright. Give us your best shot.

JOSIE What if it goes off?

TEDDY Then I'll look fucking stupid, won't I?

She levels the gun at him. He doesn't move.

TEDDY ...

JOSIE ...

You ain't scared, are you?

He smiles. She smiles.

Bang bang – you're dead.

So – Lightning Luke – you ready to go rustlin'?

TEDDY Yes, ma'am.

JOSIE Good – let's be outaws.

JOSIE pockets the gun.

She leaves.

TEDDY *follows.*

JOHNNY VALENTINE
    COS I'M READY, TEDDY, READY TO GO
    READY, TEDDY, READY TO GO
    GIVE ME ROCK 'N' ROLL AND NICE, FAST BEAT
    COS I'M READY TEDDY
    READY GO
    READY TEDDY READY GO
    READY TEDDY READY – GO!

Blackout.

Interval

Side B

JOHNNY VALENTINE Hey Buster, let's try something out. Go with me.

SONG: "BACK OF MY CADILLAC"

JOHNNY VALENTINE
>WELL THE RADIO IS PLAYING LOW AND THE STARS ARE SHININ' BRIGHT
>THE COAST WAS CLEAR WHEN WE CAME UP HERE, THERE WEREN'T A SOUL IN SIGHT
>
>**JENNY O'MALLEY** *enters.* **JOHNNY VALENTINE** *sings to her.*
>SO SCOOT OVER HERE AND IN YOUR EAR I'LL SAY WHAT YOU MEAN TO ME
>IN THE MIDNIGHT HOUR YOU CAN BE MY FLOWER I CAN BE YOUR HONEY BEE
>
>THERE'S ROOM FOR TWO IN THE BACK OF MY CADILLAC
>BABY ME AND YOU WE CAN GO TO HEAVEN AND BACK
>AIN'T NO SIN IN GOING FOR A SPIN
>TAKE A LITTLE RIDE TONIGHT

JENNY O'MALLEY
>NOW WAIT A SEC, YOU GOT NO RESPECT, I'M A LADY YES SIREE
>I AIN'T INTO THAT STUFF, ENOUGH'S ENOUGH NOW KINDLY LET ME BE
>HUGGIN', CUDDLIN', MESSIN', MUDDLIN' LEAVES ME ALL CONFUSED
>WHO KNOWS WHAT I'D DO WITH A BOY LIKE YOU AND WHAT I'D LIKELY LOSE

SAMMY "THE STICKS" SMITH *enters during this chorus and begins playing during the next verse.*

BOTH
> THERE'S ROOM FOR TWO IN THE BACK OF MY CADILLAC
> BABY ME AND YOU WE CAN GO TO HEAVEN AND BACK
> AIN'T NO SIN IN GOING FOR SPIN
> TAKE A LITTLE RIDE TONIGHT

JOHNNY VALENTINE
> NOW HOLD ON A SEC, WEREN'T IT YOU WHO SUGGESTED WE GO FOR A RIDE

JENNY O'MALLEY
> WELL MAYBE I DID

JOHNNY VALENTINE
> SO COME ON THEN KID, WHAT HAVE YOU GOT TO HIDE

JENNY O'MALLEY
> NOW EASY BOY, I AIN'T BEING COY, I'M KINDA SHOCKED, IS THAT CLEAR?

JOHNNY VALENTINE
> SURE IS MA'AM

JENNY O'MALLEY
> HELL YES, GODDAM, NOW GET YOUR ASS OVER HERE!

BAND
> THERE'S ROOM FOR TWO IN THE BACK OF MY CADILLAC
> BABY ME AND YOU WE CAN GO TO HEAVEN AND BACK
> AIN'T NO SIN IN GOING FOR SPIN
> TAKE A LITTLE RIDE TONIGHT

(Repeat chorus)

SONG: "HEARTACHE EXPRESS"

BAND
> OOOH

JOHNNY VALENTINE
> THERE'S A TRAIN A-COMING DOWN THE TRACK

I CAN HEAR ITS CHIMNEY STACK
AND I CAN HEAR ITS WAILIN' WHISTLE HIGH (WOO)
AND THOSE WHEELS THEY KEEP A-TURNIN'
MY HEART MUST START A-LEARNIN'
THAT MY BABY HAS GONE BYE-BYE

BAND

HEARTACHE EXPRESS
HEARTACHE EXPRESS
I CAN'T AFFORD THE FEE
BECAUSE MY MONEY'S MORE THAN LESS
ALL ABOARD THE
HEARTACHE EXPRESS
HEARTACHE EXPRESS

JOHNNY VALENTINE

YOU TOOK MY BABY DOWN THE TRACK
AND YOU LEFT ME IN A MESS

WELL THESE TRAIN TRACK TEARS RUN DOWN MY CHEEKS
FOR IT HAS BEEN A WHOLE SIX WEEKS
SINCE I EMBRACED MY CHERIE AMOUR
AND NOW MY ARMS ARE EMPTY
AND MY TROUBLES ARE A-PLENTY
FOR SHE AIN'T NEVER COMING BACK NO MORE

BAND

HEARTACHE EXPRESS
HEARTACHE EXPRESS
I CAN'T AFFORD THE FEE
BECAUSE MY MONEY'S MORE THAN LESS
ALL ABOARD THE
HEARTACHE EXPRESS
HEARTACHE EXPRESS

JOHNNY VALENTINE

YOU TOOK MY BABY DOWN THE TRACK
AND YOU LEFT ME IN A MESS

BAND

OOOH ETC..

JOHNNY VALENTINE
AND NOW SHE'S IN THE CITY
WHERE A GAL AS YOUNG AND PRETTY AS MY SWEETHEART
IS BOUND TO MAKE A MINT
AND LORDY KNOWS I TRIED
TO KEEP HER BY MY SIDE
BUT A GUY CAN'T KEEP A GIRL WHEN HE'S SKINT
ALL ABOARD THE...

BAND
HEARTACHE EXPRESS
HEARTACHE EXPRESS
I CAN'T AFFORD THE FEE
BECAUSE MY MONEY'S MORE THAN LESS
ALL ABOARD THE
HEARTACHE EXPRESS
HEARTACHE EXPRESS

JOHNNY VALENTINE
YOU TOOK MY BABY DOWN THE TRACK
AND YOU LEFT ME IN A MESS

BAND
OOH...

JOHNNY VALENTINE How we all doin' out there tonight? You people ready for a lil' more?

Cheers from audience...hopefully.

Well, ain't you a lively bunch? Looks like you was wrong, Sammy.

SAMMY "THE STICKS" SMITH Say what?

JOHNNY VALENTINE Sammy here told me folks in England were gonna be all stuck up, stiff and none too friendly.

SAMMY "THE STICKS" SMITH I ain't never said that.

JOHNNY VALENTINE Well, what did you say?

SAMMY "THE STICKS" SMITH I said the English fellas weren't the friendly type.

JOHNNY VALENTINE What about the English ladies?

SAMMY "THE STICKS" SMITH Oh, they been more than friendly to me so far.

JENNY O'MALLEY And that's why we keep him behind a cage where he belongs.

SAMMY "THE STICKS" SMITH What you sayin', Jenny?

JENNY O'MALLEY You best keep your mouth clean and your eyes straight ahead, else I'm gonna be teaching you a lesson you're never gonna be able to forget. You hear me?

SAMMY "THE STICKS" SMITH Yes, ma'am.

JOHNNY VALENTINE Man, you got a mean mouth on you, Jenny.

JENNY O'MALLEY Meanest there is.

JOHNNY VALENTINE You don't take shit from nobody, do you?

JENNY O'MALLEY Never have, never will.

JOHNNY VALENTINE Man, that's what I love about rock 'n' roll, ladies and gentlemen: it don't take shit from nobody.

   SONG: "OUTLAW ON THE RUN"

   DON'T YOU MESS WITH ME, BOY, IF YOU KNOW WHAT I MEAN
   I'M THE MEANEST MAN ALIVE THAT YOU EVER DONE SEEN
   YOU LOOK AT ME TWICE I'M GONNA SHOOT YOU DOWN
   I LEFT A MAN DEAD IN EVERY TOWN

   I'M AN OUTLAW ON THE RUN
   I'M AN OUTLAW ON THE RUN
   I'M AN OUTLAW ON THE RUN
   I'M AN OUTLAW ON THE RUN
   I'M AN ICE-COLD KILLER AND A REAL BAD BUCK
   IF YOU CROSS ME, BOY, THEN YOU OUTTA LUCK

   JOSIE *and* **TEDDY** *have re-entered.*

TEDDY Out of the alley and back on the street we walk shoulder to shoulder, bolder than we were before.

JOSIE Up Blackwood.

TEDDY Morcombe.

JOSIE Browning.

TEDDY Charleston Street.

JOSIE Past slumped and hunchbacked houses, wheezing gaffs.

TEDDY The fogged-up windows of steaming, grease-soaked caffs.

JOSIE Through hazy crowds that hang in the air like drizzle. Grey-faced and dreary, backs bent and weary, with a vinegar glare that'd chill the piss in the pot. But we just carry on silent and smilin', our eyes linin' up potential marks to hit. The bookie's?

TEDDY Rookie's mistake – they'll be expectin', what with all that dough. A pub?

JOSIE Too packed. What we need is something simple.

TEDDY Something small.

JOSIE Out the way where any call for help would go unheard.

TEDDY We prowl, patient, intent.

JOSIE Waiting for the perfect opportunity to present itself.

TEDDY And lo –

JOSIE – and behold –

TEDDY – it does. A pawn shop, black and battered like an old leather trunk, piles of junk pack the windows thick with yellow dust, and a battered, tattered sign that still reads "Open".

JOSIE Open late for a Saturday night but things being how they are and belts being tight, there's always business to be had for a fella like him. Plenty of cash to be had.

TEDDY I mean, it's daylight robbery already, innit? Preyin' on the poor – that desperate lot tryna keep the wolf from the door. That ain't an honest way to make a livin'.

JOSIE All we'd be doin' is takin' back, restorin' the balance, givin' the cash where it's most sorely needed. I mean – that's what outlaws do, in't it?

JOHNNY VALENTINE
DONE TEN TO TWELVE INSIDE THE STATE PEN
SOON AS I CAME OUT THEY PUT ME BACK AGAIN
I BROKE ME LOOSE AND I GOT ME A GUN, I STOLE ME A CAR
AND NOW I'M ON THE RUN

I'M AN OUTLAW ON THE RUN
I'M AN OUTLAW ON THE RUN
I'M AN OUTLAW ON THE RUN
I'M AN OUTLAW ON THE RUN
I'M AN ICE-COLD KILLER AND A REAL BAD BUCK
IF YOU CROSS ME, BOY, THEN YOU OUTTA LUCK

TEDDY The air is old and musty, the carpet worn, the walls are pale and peeling.

JOSIE And at the end amongst a row of clocks –

TEDDY – and radios, old lamps and a box of pipes and lighters, fire grates –

JOSIE – Chinese lamps and china plates –

TEDDY – family silver –

JOSIE – watches –

TEDDY – wedding rings and a million other assorted things –

JOSIE – sits a crumpled geezer in a crumpled suit, a fag glued between thin cracked lips, rheumy eyes behind gold-wire rims.

TEDDY "We're closin' up"
– he says in a tar-dipped husk.

JOSIE 'S okay, we won't be long.

TEDDY "Ain't you heard what I said?"

– and looks up. His skin is sallow, stubble-flecked and wrecked and riddled with pockmarks, a faint moustache tries to cover his lip.

"What you want?"

JOSIE Got sump'n to sell.

TEDDY "We're closed."

JOSIE Sign says you ain't.

TEDDY "I ain't turned it yet."

JOSIE Well, you can turn it when we've gone.

TEDDY "I don't want no trouble."

JOSIE That's lucky – neither do we.

TEDDY "Well – what is it?"

JOSIE We'll show you.

JOSIE *pulls out the gun.*

TEDDY "Where'd you get that?"

JOSIE Got it with a box of Cornflakes. You reckon it's worth a few bob? We'll take cash if that's alright. Where's the cash box?

TEDDY His eyes dart beneath the cabinet –

JOSIE Grab the box.

TEDDY – she says and I soon turn up a tin, bruised and battered and jangling full to the brim with coin.

JOSIE Open it!

TEDDY It's locked. Where's the key?

JOSIE Where's the fuckin' key, granddad?

TEDDY "I – I –"

JOSIE What? Speak up!

TEDDY "I – I –"

JOSIE Keys!

TEDDY She grabs the keys from his cracked and wind-chapped fists, flings them cross the counter, I catch it, find the right one, turn the latch, it pops and from its guts falls coin and notes, floatin' to the floor.

There's gotta be ten quid in there.

JOSIE No time to count it.

TEDDY I clutch it. Stuff it pocket-deep.

JOSIE Keep movin'. Won't be long 'fore someone stumble's in and finds us.

TEDDY The cash collected, place inspected for more immediate valuables, we turn and to the door make haste to our escape before he calls out from the floor –

"Fuckin' kids."

Music stops.

JOSIE ...

What was that?

Bass continues.

TEDDY "You think you scare me? You don't scare me none. I seen that gun before. The War. Seen Krauts as big as tanks come full pelt at me with that clutched in their fist. You think some punk and Judie, rudely bargin' in and playin' cowboy gonna make me shit a brick? If I were half my age, I'd wipe that smile clean off your face."

JOSIE You wanna have a go, old man? Keep talking.

TEDDY "You and your lot, sonny –"

– he phlegms at me with a fixed stare –

"– ain't gonna scare me none with your pop guns and your switchblades and your slick-back hair, cos underneath the swish and brag and swagger there's nothin' bigger than a little boy."

What you say?

"Fuck me, thought I was the deaf one round here."

Say it again.

"Then listen closely, boy, cos you and your little slut here – you're nothin' but a pair of fuckin' kids."

Music stops.

She takes the pistol, swings it high and lands the butt on his head. Red pours from the wound and whimpers from his lips as he falls back again and slips onto the floor, pawing at his bleeding crown.

JOSIE Watch your fucking language, grandpa – there's ladies present.

TEDDY Yeah, show a bit of respect, you silly old fuck.

Music continues.

She laughs hard, grabs my hand and we both duck out into the street, our feet in syncopated time rapping concrete with jazzy basslines, two at a time, pounding pavement and breathless, elated and weightless at our daring heist.

JOHNNY VALENTINE
    I'M AN OUTLAW ON THE RUN
    I'M AN OUTLAW ON THE RUN
    I'M AN OUTLAW ON THE RUN
    I'M AN OUTLAW ON THE RUN
    I'M AN ICE-COLD KILLER AND A REAL BAD BUCK
    IF YOU CROSS ME, BOY, THEN YOU OUTTA LUCK

End of song.

JOSIE We don't stop till the shop and its occupant are a distant memory, and now crouched behind a chippy, amongst discarded potato peels and vinegar reek, we check our takings.

TEDDY Nine pound, shilling and six pence.

JOSIE Such immense wealth blows our minds.

TEDDY We could see Johnny twenty times over and still have cash to burn.

JOSIE Our pockets plush with cash we set out on foot –

Slow blues riff.

Nah, fuck that, we catch a cab.

Fast blues riff.

We got the coin to spare – and ride in style towards our evening's goal, namely: Teddy's.

TEDDY It's round the back of Penton Place, a cramped and grimy alley, invisible – the only clue the queue outside headed by a six-foot man-monolith who stands outside and stares at you from his one good eye (the other shrapnel shot and lost in a bank raid ten years ago, so the stories go), guarding entry to its treasures for any chancer who thinks that the pleasure of music and a dance don't come with a price.

"What you want?"

Music fades.

– he says.

JOSIE A cup o' tea and a sit down – what you think?

TEDDY "Don't be funny with me, sunshine – I ain't the laughin' type."

JOSIE We wanna come in.

TEDDY "Entry ain't cheap – how much pocket money you reckon you got, little girl?"

JOSIE "Plenty," I says and fly two filthy great pound notes before his face like flags and coo, "Now, can we come in – please?"

TEDDY He grunts, clearly miffed but since presented with incontrovertible dough, he must concede and grumbles low –

"Alright – in you go."

JOSIE We head down a dim stairwell, flaked with peeling posters and deep into the belly of Teddy's.

TEDDY The place is a dive but fuck me if it ain't shakin'. It's liver-red and tiger-striped, taps at the bar pissing beer for a hundred, hundred Teds and Judies crammed in together, quiffs to the ceiling, hot enough to make the walls sweat.

JOSIE The jukebox is jumpin' and ready to burst, but the crowd keeps on kickin'. It's so tight in there you barely know who's dancing with who, people holding onto each other real tight just so's they won't drown.

TEDDY Already there's sweat on the back of my neck and my top lip. The thick air's pulling down on my quiff – thank fuck I've got the thing greased like an engine. But my leg's shaking and my feet are twitchin'.

JOSIE Itchin' already to jitter and groove, move like lightnin', but I'm fightin' the urge to move just now cos the real deal, the real business ain't even started yet.

TEDDY We head to the bar, shoulder our way through the crowd, so loud I can barely hear myself when I order two pints, which turn up blood-warm and foaming, bitter and brooding, sling the barman our stolen coppers, prop ourselves against the wood and watch the room.

JOSIE When all of a sudden the lights extinguish –

TEDDY – the stage is plunged into darkness –

JOSIE – and I realise that it's upon us –

TEDDY He's here.

Snare roll.

JENNY O'MALLEY Ladies and gentlemen. Live from his sell-out performance at the Trocadero this very night. He's not done rockin'. He's not done rollin'. In fact he's still got a whole lotta shakin' to do for you. Are you ready? You best be ready to give it up for the Casanova of Cool. The Romeo of Rhythm. The one, the only: Johnny Valentine & The Broken Hearts.

JOHNNY VALENTINE *appears. It is as if the Morning Star itself has arrived onstage.*

JOHNNY VALENTINE How y'all doin' tonight? You folks ready for a little rock 'n' roll? Yeah – you look about ready to me. Let's do this thing.

SONG: "DANCE OFF THE BLUES"
YOU BROKE MY HEART AND LEFT ME BLUE
I DIDN'T HAVE A CHANCE
BUT THERE'S ONE THING THAT'LL GET ME THROUGH
GOTTA GET TO MY FEET AND DANCE DANCE DANCE

WELL-A DANCE, DANCE, DANCE OFF THE BLUES
SHIMMY SHIMMY HARD AND SHAKE YOUR SHOES
I SAID, DANCE, DANCE, DANCE TILL YOU DROP
DO THE OOGIE BOOGIE WOOGIE AND THE HOT FLIP-FLOP
YEAH, DANCE, DANCE, DANCE ALL NIGHT
I DANCE SO FAST MY FEET CATCH ALIGHT
DANCE, DANCE, DANCE OFF THE BLUES
MOVE YOUR BODY, BABY, I GOT NOTHIN' TO LOSE
OOOOOH HELP ME!

Music continues.

TEDDY Jesus –

JOSIE – fucking –

TEDDY – Christ!

JOSIE The crowd goes from nought to sixty in seconds, beckoned on by the silver-tongue god standing on stage and in a mad instant, passion and rage spark the gunpowder in our guts and the whole room does everything short of explode and goes completely fucking nuts!

TEDDY Heads start a boppin', knees flip-floppin', elbows poppin' out like the pistons of some insane machine. And the voices – the screams!

JOSIE Banshee wailin' and tongues flailin' about like whips across bright-red lips as hoots, whoops and hollers shoot up and pop the collars that cling to their throats as bellowing notes burst from their throats and rev like engines.

TEDDY But over it all, proud and tall, his voice as loud as a goddamn cannonball stands Johnny Valentine, his face all a-shine with sweat, his hips petrol-powered and swinging, his body jumpin', he just keeps on singin' as if he was born to do nothin' else in the whole goddamn world and I look at him up there on that stage like a god and I think, "Oh my God – that could be – one, some distant day from now, that could be –"

JOSIE Let's go!

TEDDY What?

JOSIE You heard me – let's dance.

JOHNNY VALENTINE
A-ONE, A-TWO, A-ONE, TWO, THREE, FOUR.

They dance. It's wild and joyful, barely contained.

BAND
BLUES, BLUES, DANCE OFF THE BLUES
BLUES, BLUES, DANCE OFF THE BLUES ETC...

JOHNNY VALENTINE
I SAID A-DANCE, DANCE, DANCE OFF THE BLUES
SHIMMY SHIMMY HARD AND SHAKE YOUR SHOES
I SAID, DANCE, DANCE, DANCE TILL YOU DROP
DO THE OOGIE BOOGIE WOOGIE AND THE HOT FLIP-FLOP
YEAH, DANCE, DANCE, DANCE ALL NIGHT
I DANCE SO FAST MY FEET CATCH ALIGHT
DANCE, DANCE, DANCE OFF THE BLUES
MOVE YOUR BODY, BABY

MOVE YOUR BODY, BABY
I SAID A-MOVE YOUR BODY, BABY
I SAID A-MOVE YOUR BODY, BABY, I GOT NOTHING TO LOSE!

TEDDY *lifts and dips* **JOSIE** *and they hang suspended – the whole world seems to freeze in that moment – before gravity kicks back in and breathless they come crashing feet first back to the floor.*

End of song.

They stand exhausted but elated, panting and sweating.

They look at each other. They smile.

Well I think we've been cookin' up a storm in here, cool cats and hot dogs, don't you think? How 'bout we take it down for a moment? Nice and low, soft and slow.

They slow dance.

SONG: "BLUE WITH OUT YOU".

MY DARLING, MY DEAREST, I LONG FOR YOUR TOUCH
MY DARLING LOVE, I MISS YOU SO MUCH
PLEASE COME BACK TO ME, CAN'T YOU SEE
I DON'T KNOW WHAT TO DO

COS I'M BLUE
BLUE WITHOUT YOU

I'M BEGGIN' YOU, BABY, DOWN ON MY KNEES
FOR YOU TO COME BACK TO ME
SAY YOU WILL PLEASE
I AM IN DISTRESS, MY MIND'S A MESS
AND MY HEART IS BROKEN IN TWO

COS I'M BLUE
BLUE WITHOUT YOU

WITHOUT YOUR LOVIN'
THE SKIES ARE DARK AND BLACK
THE BIRDS HAVE LEFT THEIR SONG
THE SUN HAS GONE AND TURNED HIS BACK

WE BELONG TOGETHER, YOU AND I
TOGETHER FOREVER TILL THE END OF TIME
BUT IF YOU STAY GONE, IT WON'T BE LONG
TILL I'M DONE AND FINISHED AND THROUGH

COS I'M BLUE
BLUE WITHOUT YOU

COS I'M BLUE
BLUE WITHOUT YOU

YES I'M BLUE
BLUE WITHOUT YOU

They kiss. It might be the greatest kiss ever.

TEDDY ...

JOSIE ...

JOHNNY VALENTINE We're gonna take a little break – powder our noses, whet our whistles and whatnot, but this'll be goin' on all night long, don't you worry. We'll see you for more hot music in five, meantime – stay cool.

TEDDY ...

JOSIE ...

TEDDY You're a good dancer.

JOSIE You ain't so bad yourself.

TEDDY I could use a drink.

JOSIE Me too.

TEDDY You wanna a beer?

JOSIE Yeah. I do.

TEDDY Two beers, comin' up.

JOSIE Sounds good.

TEDDY Won't be long.

JOSIE Better not be. I'll be waitin' here.

TEDDY Best catch your breath.

JOSIE Oh yeah?

TEDDY You're gonna need it.

JOSIE ...

TEDDY ...

> I turn – head last, for one more look – then brook the flow of bodies at the bar, slither through, order two more beers – think about her waitin' on the dance floor and take my eyes off the drinks for a second – for just one second – and turn too quickly and smack into a Ted, spilling two pints of piss-warm beer all down his threads.
>
> Fuck me, mate, can't you –
>
> He's a barrel-broad bastard at least six foot seven, with the quiff – I never seen nothing like it. It's like the prow of a battleship. Granite face with ink-black eyes and a broad, bulbous and recently broken nose.

JOSIE "What the fuck is this? What you fucking done? You any fucking idea how much this cost? It's in my fucking shoes as well."

TEDDY "What's this bastard gone and done, Tully?" a thin and sneering voice enquires.

JOSIE "He's gone and done a right stupid fucking thing."

TEDDY – this Tully says and it dawns on me that this is the self-same groping gorilla who tried to cop a feel of my lovely Smiler way back when in the Coronet earlier tonight.

> Oh fuck.

JOSIE "You just ruined my shirt, you blind bastard. Ain't you got nothin' to say to me?"

TEDDY I'm speechless, my tongue made lead by the sight of his inked fists like anvils. But I think about his greasy grip all over her earlier tonight and my heart, before racing from fear, now anger, begins to beat faster and I say –

You wanna watch where you're goin', mate.

JOSIE "You what?"

TEDDY You heard.

JOSIE "Wait a minute – I remember you. The scrawny little fuck who tried his luck back up at the Church. Looks like you owe me a double apology."

TEDDY I don't owe you shit.

JOSIE "Now, now."

TEDDY Fuck you.

JOSIE "I'll only ask you nicely once, you lanky streak of piss. Apologise."

TEDDY Make me.

His hand, thick as rope, goes for my throat and lifts me clean in the air. My toes skitter against the floor, dangling like a hanging man. I can't breathe. I can't fucking breathe.

JOSIE Suddenly, there's a rumble at the bar, I turn and see the gathered crowd pull back and gasp and I see flying past and pinned to the wall like an insect under inspection is a fella, who looks – it's him, my Smiler! And the thick tattooed grip around his neck belongs to none other than Tully, ugly as ever and twice as pissed off.

"Listen here, you boy, you spick, you speck,"

– he says –

"I said apologise and you will fucking apologise. Do you get me?"

TEDDY His free hand fishes into his pocket and pulls out a stiletto.

JOSIE He's got a knife.

TEDDY He presses the thin and angry blade against my eye.

JOSIE Oh fuck.

TEDDY I can't breathe.

JOSIE Oh fuck, I gotta –

TEDDY I can't –

JOSIE – do summit, I gotta –

TEDDY I –

JOSIE Thoughtless, I grab a glass and crash it hard 'gainst his head, cocksure that I could once again bring this Goliath to the ground. But although I knew this fella was stupid, I weren't prepared for him to be so thick skulled, for the effect of my attack is next to nil.

"Fuck me, if ain't my chickadee!"

– he says, surprised and somewhat delighted that he'll be granted a chance to repay the favour of a broken nose which he does with a backhand that lands square 'gainst my face and sends me flying floor-wards –

"Found yourself a new fella real quick, didn't ya? Tully no good for you, was he? If there's one thing I can't stand it's a stuck-up, choosey floozy."

– and upwards lifts a boot whose route must surely end upon my face –

TEDDY Blinded and breathless, I forward-spring and shoulder his ribs.

JOSIE – but nothing comes – instead he's thrown aside.

TEDDY I take a swing but he feints and I come up with nothing but air. I trip, grip desperate at the bar and scrabble at the beer-soaked floor but he's on me, grabs my scruffs and roughly drags me and slams me down.

JOSIE With him pinned to the bar, Tully picks up a pint and holding it high pours it over his hair and face.

TEDDY I'm blinded by beer and pomade. I can't breathe, I can't see. My arms swing wildly before I'm dragged up and thrown down on the floor.

JOSIE He's wet and gasping like a landed fish, and then Tully steps over him and kneels down, pinning his chest to the floor with his leg.

TEDDY I feel like I've got a mountain on me. He reaches for my hair – my luscious curls once quiffed and quaffed, now sodden and dripping in my eye – and wraps a thick knot of it round his fingers, lifts his blade and grimly smiling says –

JOSIE "Something for the weekend, sir?"

– before he hacks at his forelock and tears it off like he's scalped him and he screams like a scratched record.

TEDDY I try to cry out again but he leans in close, the weight of him squeezing all the air out of my body and he whispers like a snake –

JOSIE "Now you sit tight while I'll pluck me a few feathers from your little dolly bird. Don't say a word, don't struggle. Just sit and watch and behave yourself like a good – little – boy."

TEDDY The last word dropped like fag ash in my eyes, he smiles then rises, turns and there he finds –

JOSIE *points the gun and shoots Tully.*

TEDDY ...

JOSIE ...

You'd never've thought such a small thing could make such a noise. Everyone's amazed, stood silent in shock, not least of all Tully. He's wide-eyed, surprised – maybe not so much at the noise as the hole in his neck which bubbles blood. He tries to speak and his windpipe whistles useless. He coughs and splutters, mutters something incomprehensible then falls face first at my feet, blood pooling round my shoes, 'cross the floor.

The noise that comes next is pretty big too – maybe cos of the silence before. Two hundred people – maybe more – all screaming in panic, manically making for the exit, glass shattered, drinks splattered, tables and chairs tossed aside with no care about who's gonna clean up this mess.

And in amongst of the fleeing feet, I see him lain on the floor – clothes rough and torn, head freshly shorn, and on his face no more that familiar smile but a look of surprise. Everyone looks so surprised.

I think it works.

TEDDY ...

JOSIE ...

TEDDY "Name?"

JOSIE Josie.

TEDDY Teddy.

JOSIE "Age?"

TEDDY Eighteen.

JOSIE Seventeen.

TEDDY "Occupation?"

JOSIE Shop girl.

TEDDY Junker.

JOSIE "Family?"

TEDDY Mother.

JOSIE Mum and Dad.

TEDDY "Do they know you're here? How bad things have got?"

JOSIE "I mean, who knows if they'll come for you or not?"

TEDDY I – I don't know.

JOSIE Don't care.

TEDDY "Well you should."

JOSIE "Cos things ain't lookin' good."

TEDDY "I mean, we got a room full of witnesses say they saw her –"

JOSIE "Say they saw you pull the gun."

TEDDY "But what I wanna know is –"

JOSIE "Where d'you get it from? Was it him?"

TEDDY "Was it her? Son, I give you my word, if you testify that she coerced you, the worst you'd be looking at it is six months – twelve at tops."

JOSIE "Cos if it's him that brought it, it ought to be him that shares the guilt. What's done is done, blood's spilt – but it don't have be just your hands what is red."

TEDDY "But if I ain't said it before, let me explain sump'n: if you stay silent, the judge will see nothin' but a violent thug hell-bent on thrills and hard liquor, and you'll be sent quicker than you can think to the clink for a very long time. And where you're goin' it ain't for kids. You ain't in the school yard no more."

JOSIE "I mean, who knows when you'll next see the light of day."

TEDDY "And what about your mum? How come you ain't thought about her yet? Cos I'll bet what with you locked away forever and a day and with nobody left, the poor old darlin'll be bereft and a broken heart don't live long. Alone, abandoned, no hope, no son. You reckon she can take any more heartbreak?"

JOSIE "So why don't you tell us what really happened?"

TEDDY "Tell us what really went down."

JOSIE "Cos it's him or you."

TEDDY "It's you or her."

JOSIE ...

TEDDY ...

JOSIE "No?"

TEDDY "Nothing?"

JOSIE "Alright then."

TEDDY "Tell you what."

JOSIE "I'm gonna leave you to have a think."

TEDDY "And think long and hard, cos this might be the biggest decision you ever make."

JOSIE ...

TEDDY ...

JOSIE That was hours ago.

TEDDY I think. I lost track of time.

JOSIE No window.

TEDDY No clock.

JOSIE Nothin' to look at but four walls and a locked door.

TEDDY My scalp is burning with pain and shame. My wrists too. They're sore.

JOSIE The chaffing cuffs cutting red raw bracelets into my skin.

TEDDY And their chains tinkle and make a little music.

JOSIE Alone and sitting in silence.

TEDDY Just four grey walls and me.

JOSIE The only colour another man's blood on my shoes.

TEDDY I think about my house. My home.

JOSIE It's round the corner from here, but it's further away than it's ever been before.

TEDDY The threadbare carpet.

JOSIE The tea-stained kitchen table.

TEDDY Two lifeless marigolds wetly dangling in the sink.

JOSIE The gin-soaked doily.

TEDDY The lifeless wireless.

JOSIE My father and mother upstairs asleep in separate beds.

TEDDY Mum coiled up on the tear-soaked, worn-out couch.

JOSIE Dad's workcoat hanging limply behind the kitchen door.

TEDDY I wonder if she made it upstairs tonight?

JOSIE Waiting for Monday morning.

TEDDY How she'll make it upstairs if I ain't there.

JOSIE To start the whole fucking week again.

TEDDY I think –

JOSIE I think –

TEDDY I need to sleep.

JOSIE I'm tired.

TEDDY My room.

JOSIE My bed. My Thompson six stack, the plastic cracked and the red paint flaking, waiting in the corner.

TEDDY Six platters packed one on top of the other, ready to sing at the flick of a switch and the turn of a crank.

JOSIE Gene Vincent, Buddy Holly.

TEDDY Old Hank.

JOSIE Lovely Johnny Valentine.

MUSIC: "BLUE WITHOUT YOU – REPRISE"

TEDDY I close my eyes and listen, hear that static pop and crackle and see the vinyl glisten in its lazy turns beneath the light hanging overhead.

JOSIE And lying on my bed, I can hear those big blue notes bloom, one by one, and slowly fill the room.

TEDDY And it's our song.

JOSIE Our song.

JOHNNY VALENTINE *(under dialogue)*
  MY DARLIN' MY DEAREST I LONG FOR YOUR TOUCH

TEDDY The tempo slow, melody cool and long.

JOSIE The bass beneath a soft heartbeat.

TEDDY I lie and listen, the notes roll over me, swell, drag and hush.

JOSIE The soft sandy shush of the song swallows me and then lifts me up to my feet.

TEDDY Wraps me in its arms.

JOSIE I look up.

TEDDY And I see –

JOSIE It's him.

JOHNNY VALENTINE *(under dialogue)*
  MY DARLIN' LOVE I MISS YOU SO MUCH

TEDDY It's her. Her hands hang from my neck.

JOSIE Around my waist.

TEDDY Those same red lips.

JOSIE That same soft face and two blue burning eyes.

TEDDY We're back at Teddy's.

JOSIE The place is empty now except us. The jukebox in the corner glows blood-red.

TEDDY The light from the mirrorball overhead.

JOSIE I hold him close and think –

TEDDY Just after this –

JOSIE We'll run away. Like we said we would.

TEDDY Grab a plane, take off, head west.

JOHNNY VALENTINE *(under dialogue)*
PLEASE COME BACK TO ME, CAN'T YOU SEE
I DON'T KNOW WHAT TO DO

JOSIE California's best, we agree.

TEDDY Cross the blue to a new life.

JOSIE Whatever we want.

TEDDY New names, new faces.

JOSIE Places we've never seen outside of magazines will fall beneath the wheels of our new Cadillac.

TEDDY Cherry-red paintwork.

JOSIE Six-cylinder engine.

TEDDY Chrome wingtip lights and leather interior.

JOSIE Black.

TEDDY People will stare at us, we drive past, jaws on the floor beneath their feet.

JOSIE And we'll drive so fucking fast it'll make your head spin.

JOHNNY VALENTINE *(under dialogue)*
COS I'M BLUE
BLUE WITHOUT YOU

TEDDY But let's just stay here for a while.

JOSIE For a little bit a least.

TEDDY Just here.

JOSIE And finish this dance.

TEDDY Finish this song.

JOSIE I'm pretty sure it won't take long.

They slow dance.

JOHNNY VALENTINE
WITHOUT YOUR LOVIN'

THE SKIES ARE DARK AND BLACK
THE BIRDS HAVE LOST THEIR SONG
THE SUN HAS GONE AND TURNED HIS BACK

Suddenly, they are each back in their cells – alone.

BAND *(a cappella)*
WE BELONG TOGETHER
YOU AND I
TOGETHER FOREVER TILL THE END OF TIME
BUT IF YOU STAY GONE
IT WON'T BE LONG
TILL I'M DONE AND FINISHED AND THROUGH

COS I'M BLUE
BLUE WITHOUT YOU

COS I'M BLUE
BLUE WITHOUT YOU

YES I'M BLUE
BLUE WITHOUT YOU

End

THIS IS NOT THE END

Visit samuelfrench.co.uk and discover the best theatre bookshop on the internet

A vast range of plays
Acting and theatre books
Gifts

samuelfrench.co.uk

samuelfrenchltd

samuel french uk

www.ingramcontent.com/pod-product-compliance
Lightning Source LLC
LaVergne TN
LVHW051706080426
835511LV00017B/2762